PERCEPTIONS
GARY BECK

This publication is a creative work protected in full by all applicable copyright laws, as well as by misappropriation, trade secret, unfair competition, and other applicable laws. No part of this book may be reproduced or transmitted in any manner without written permission from Winter Goose Publishing, except in the case of brief quotations embodied in critical articles or reviews. All rights reserved.

Winter Goose Publishing
45 Lafayette Road #114
North Hampton, NH 03862

www.wintergoosepublishing.com
Contact Information: info@wintergoosepublishing.com

Perceptions

COPYRIGHT © 2016 by Gary Beck

First Edition, June, 2016

Cover Design by Winter Goose Publishing
Typesetting by Odyssey Books

ISBN: 978-1-941058-49-7

Published in the United States of America

"Les Fenêtres
A renaître, portant mon rêve en diadème,
Au ciel antérieur où fleurit la Beauté!"

—Stéphane Mallarmé

Contents

Anthem	1
The Changing World	2
Companions	4
Iraq Monologues	5
Ode to Loss	12
Diminishing Mass	13
Excursion	14
House Finch	15
Arsonist's Dream	16
Original Sin	17
Girl Soldier	18
Don't Look Back	20
Paradox	21
Non-Renewable	22
Physicist's Fantasy	23
The Evil That Men Do	24
Misunderstood	25
Headlines	27
Empire State Building	28
Great Beginnings	31
Brute Force	33
Orbit	34
Progress	35
Dependency	36
Encroachment	37
Light at the End of . . .	38
Globalization	41
Resourceful	42

Battered Republic	43
Paradox II	44
Evolving Education	46
Future War	47
Diagnosis	49
Shadows	50
To Rejected Suitors Who Can't Take No for an Answer	51
Survival	52
Harsh Change	53
No Saviors	54
The End of . . .	55
Paradox III	56
Fixed Positions	60
Denial Is Cheaper	61
Astral Gap	62
Art History	63
Night Patrol	66
Innovative Love	67
Across the Universe	68
Paradox IV	69
Estranged Kin	70
The Tyranny of Oil	71
Urban Oasis	72
More Light	73
Intonations of Dead Presidents	74
Us or Them	76
One More Darfur Disaster	77
Unpredictable	78
A Benefit of The Information Age	79
Paradox V	80
Dead Zones, A Poetic Explanation	81

Invocation	82
Who Will Feed Us?	83
Special Education	85
Prognosis	86
Whither Goest?	87
For Whom the Cash Flows	88
Roadside	89
What Profiteth	90
Madness Agonistes	91
Global Warming	93
Paradox VI	94
Witchcraft	95
Rampage	96
Ravenous Black Hole	97
Who Will Bear Our Burden?	98
Capital Expansion	99
Hard Times	102
Matriculation	103
Anthropology	104
Distant Ventures	106
Paranoid? Or . . .	107
A Moral Tale A La Shelley	108
A Turbulent Bird	109
The Madness of Our Times	111
Other Means	112
Cruel Capitalism	113
Paradox VII	114
Imminent Event	115
A Way of Life	117
A Progressive Nation	118
Hierarchy	119

One Solution	120
Erosive Streets	121
Oh, Too Human	122
Dereliction of Duty	123
City of Compassion	124
Ecology	125
Service	126
A Matter of . . .	127
Ode to Continuation	128
About the Author	130

"The chaos of our time is no greater than at other times, just far more dangerous."

"Poetry is the most solitary creative process of all the arts. It is also the most fragile, so far removed from large audiences and public renown that it is inexplicable why we have so many poets in America. They far outnumber engineers and chemists. Our society does not seem to have the capacity to elevate a poet to be a culture hero. So what is the role of the poet in an electronic world of instant communication? Poetry is closest to theater in ideally providing the audience with an emotional experience. But unlike theater, the poet rarely impacts well through performance, but through receptive reading. Poets once inspired, illuminated, seduced, possibly stirred to wrath, all emotional extremes that justified the exertion of the isolated artist. The movement away from live performing arts is implacable. In a superficially conditioned visual culture words cannot compete with hi-tech imagery. Nevertheless, the poet must continue to present a humanistic element in his or her creative process, otherwise the poet will become increasingly divorced from the issues of our times, and lose relevancy."

"The Evolution of Poetry"
—Gary Beck

Published by Lunar Poetry

To Carol

*A bright light that should not go gently into
the dark night, but cherish remaining time*

Anthem

The songs America once sang,
paeans to prosperity,
were only briefly interrupted
by dirges of depression,
rapidly forgotten
when the ailing economy
pleased us with recovery.

We still had hopes for tomorrow.

As the factories grow silent
unemployment lines expand,
job opportunities decline,
the service sector beckons
the liberal arts majors
who thrived in sheltered campuses,
now cast adrift on harsher streets.

We do not sing the fraying dream.

And as anticipation fades
the bitter herb of failure
pervades our damaged systems
suffering from rejections,
driving some of us to strike out
at wives, lovers, children, schools,
self-destructive blood baths.

So we lose the gift of song

The Changing World

Tensions rise across the globe
in endless confrontations
that could expedite
disastrous war.
The most dangerous threats,
weapons of mass destruction,
nuke, chem., bio.,
all promise devastation.

As the world grows smaller
differences collide
often irresolvable,
except by violence.

The United Nations,
really not united,
peacekeeping efforts
easily thwarted
by dissenting countries
whose interests are not served
in preventing genocide,
the spread of terror.

In a process of default
America became
the policeman of the world,
or select portions thereof,
the only nation
with means for intervention.

But honest citizens
as well as criminals
are suspicious of cops,
the only opposition
to cartels, rogue states, terror,
and much of the world
does not appreciate
gifts of safety,
made at horrendous cost
to our conflicted land.

Companions

We sit by the window,
my dog and I,
watching the rain.
We do not want to go out
in the torrential downpour.
He thinks doggie thoughts.
I listen to world news;
murders, suicide bombings,
natural disasters
ravaging the globe,
leaving us content
to remain indoors.

Iraq Monologues

I. G.I.

What the eff am I doing here?
Everybody hates us,
except when we give them things,
then they hate us even more.
I never know who we're fighting.
Can't tell a Sunni from a Shia.
Everyone has AK-47s,
so you never know
who's going to zap you.
The Lt. is young,
so I listen to the sarge
who always reminds me:
"Shoot if they come at you."
I want to give gum and candy,
but I'd rather waste a civilian
then go home in a body bag.

II. Sunni

I didn't have much
when Saddam ruled
and I don't have much now,
but I must always pretend
to agree with fellow Sunnis,
or they will murder me.

All I have is my olive grove
that everyone taxes;
Shia, Kurd, al-Qaeda,
the government,
even my brethren, the Sunnis.
I try to have faith in Allah
and always obey the imam,
but I can only wonder
if things will ever get better.

III. Shia

For so many years
Saddam suppressed us
and we suffered
for Allah's sake.
Now he's gone,
but the Sunni dogs
still refuse to bow
to the true belief.
Our militias can't agree
who is a friend, or enemy.
We kill each other
and blame al-Qaeda,
the American dogs,
or Syria.
We can't trust Iran,
yet we need her bombs
to kill the infidels
and false believers.

Americans must leave Iraq,
so we can kill each other
without interference.

IV. Kurd

We have always been oppressed,
Ottomans, Turks, Persians, Arabs,
all have murdered our people.
All have been our enemies,
denying us a homeland,
keeping us divided.
When the Americans
finally caught Saddam
we hoped they would help us
get a country of our own,
but they betrayed us,
as they have betrayed others
to suit their own interests
and to preserve Iraq.
Now the Turks cross the border,
attacking us with planes and tanks
and no one will defend us,
making us fear
that we will never have
a Kurdistan.

V. Al-Qaeda

The only thing sweeter
than killing Americans
are the cries of their women
lamenting in despair
the loss of their loved ones.
As long as the infidels
pollute the lands of Islam
we will give them gifts of death
from the Caliph in the mountains.
The roadside bombs
from the Iranians
delight us when they explode,
slaying unbelievers
and the dogs who serve them.
I don't know how long I'll live,
but Allah will welcome me,
because I serve his will
and kill his enemies.

VI. Mahdi Army

I know we fight
to defeat our enemies,
who are everywhere.
I don't know what to believe,
though I always praise Allah
as I do my duty
to the militia.

I obey orders,
whatever they are
and kill whoever they say,
whenever they say.
God is great.

VII. Bedouin

May they all perish,
Americans, Iraqis,
the Kurds, al-Qaeda,
all the dogs who defile
the peace of the desert.
As long as they don't find oil
beneath the spreading sands
the invaders will move on,
as invaders always do,
leaving us once again
the silence of the dunes.

VIII. British Officer

We still support the Yanks,
whether we like it or not.
They're the only ones
who maintain order
and a whiff of gunpowder
from time to time
keeps our troops sharp.

We still do a good job,
as long as it's not too big,
and we did well in Basra,
until the Mahdi army,
criminal thugs,
al-Qaeda,
ran amok,
disrupting the peace.
So we pulled back
and let the Iraqis,
backed by the Yanks,
do the dirty work
we once did ourselves
in better days,
now gone forever.

IX. Sunni Mother

When they came for my son
I begged my husband
not to let them take him.
Instead he beat me,
cursed me for being
a mere woman
who didn't understand
it was for the glory
of Allah.
Now they've come
for my only daughter,
a twelve-year-old flower

who they want to adorn
with a suicide vest.
I pleaded with my husband
to spare her,
but he beat me, cursed me,
leaving me helpless,
doubting the justice of Allah.

X. Shia Girl

Once again school is closed
and if it reopens
the religious police
will deny entry
to women.
I sit home alone
dreading my future.
My father promised me
to a rich old man
who paid him
to possess me.
I used to dream
that I'd attend
the university,
become a doctor,
heal my people.
Now hope is shattered
and I'm only left
with hatred for men.

Ode to Loss

We live as if we have
endless tomorrows
extending human sway
in blind entitlement,
legislated or believed,
that we are worthy
of continuation
despite planting and reaping
seeds of destruction,
permanently weakening
sheltering mother earth.

Diminishing Mass

I went to church on Christmas Eve
and sat with the congregation.
It could have been mosque or temple,
a gathering place of worship
where the troubled seek the divine,
while the secure display their faith.
My hope was for sincerity
hiding behind the mystery
of impenetrable faces
professing their devotion
in a religious ritual
binding people together
one night a year,
not time enough
for consolation.

Excursion

"Let's go to the beach today,"
a child asked, but was refused.
"The ultraviolet's too strong.
We'll burn, then get cancer."
"What if we cover up?"
"Exposure is dangerous.
Instead we'll go out tonight
and try to get ice cream."
"Aw, Mom. They never have any."
"Maybe they will this time."
"Aw, Mom. You always say that."
"Would you rather stay home?"
"No. I want to go out.
I hate living this way."
"Things'll get better some day."
"That's what you always say."

House Finch

I am not as bold
as other birds
and sit in fear
in fragile nest
dreading the search
for nourishment,
compelling flight
to danger zones.
The worst menace
are the sparrows
outhatching all,
intruding in
territory
once shared by all.
Now they swagger,
nasty bullies,
and I can't feed.
Pigeons, starlings,
even my kin,
the purple finch,
menace me.
I sit in fear
in fragile nest
worried that my flock
will not survive.

Arsonist's Dream

Burnt offerings
seldom appease
incendiary rage
kindled in madness
constantly smoldering,
only diverted,
temporarily,
by conflagration.

Original Sin

Everything mankind does
in the natural world
has become unnatural.
We have tainted the air,
poisoned the water,
depleted our food,
until once again
the few have much,
the many little.
The difference this time
is that equality
will assert itself
in the consumed earth
as we perish together.

Girl Soldier

A twelve-year-old girl was abducted
by the Lord's Resistance Army,
a feared Ugandan rebel group,
forced to walk hundreds of miles,
like thousands of other children
taken to secret jungle camps.

Among other things she was taught
to fire an AK-47,
then raped and treated like a slave,
laboring in the fields by day,
rarely receiving enough food.

If she protested her treatment
she was brutally beaten,
saw others beaten to death,
learned to suffer in silence.

Girls were kidnapped for special roles;
spies, porters, fighters, mine sweepers,
but mostly used as concubines
until their masters tired of them
and sent them to die in combat.

This tragic child is not unique.
Millions of African children
continue to be victims of war,
orphaned, forced from their homes, abused,

terrorized, denied education,
compelled to fight in conflicts
perpetrated by their elders.

Pleas to save the children
from human rights groups
are ignored by rebel fighters,
disputing with their government
who will exploit their battered land.

Children at an early age
are easily taught to obey,
if taken from their families
and beaten into submission.

When the community of man
cruelly abandons their offspring
we revert to primitive times
that erode civilization.

Don't Look Back

When I was young
boys still enjoyed
building snow forts,
snowball fights,
sledding,
ice skating.
Greenhouse effect
and climate change
altered winter.
At the same time
boys left the farms,
flocked to cities
and moved indoors,
plastic toys
the substitute
for outdoor play.
Video games
enslaved them,
planting youth
in front of screens
that shield them
from the future.

Paradox

It's ironic that doves,
almost as violent as hawks,
just not as rapacious,
have become the symbol of peace,
while hawks represent war.
These are convenient terms
for the simple-minded,
but a painful reminder
to wiser citizens
that we don't make an effort
to resist confusion
in this deceptive world.

Non-Renewable

I see the hopes
of my battered land
submerging,
dragged down by oil barrels.
And as the tide recedes
from our once bright future,
ebbing away brief grandeur
in conquest and defeat,
events that always meet
deciding destinies,
suborning justice,
depleting resolution
that allows survival,
our once great land
trembles at tomorrow.

Physicist's Fantasy

I never met
a Black Hole,
except in humans,
a void consuming
all the energy
that we require
to produce atoms
of continuation.

The Evil That Men Do

A warlord in eastern Congo
recruited child soldiers,
in flagrant violation
of international law.
No international police
were sent to rescue them.
The U.N. objected,
but it was only talk
and the abuses went on.
A Congolese official
blamed forces of a rebel,
Laurent Nkunda, for raiding
ten secondary schools,
four primary schools,
kidnapping students
but never specified
the standards of recruitment.
Children went to school that day
hoping to learn for tomorrow,
but did not return home that night
matriculating into sorrow.

Misunderstood

When we take military action
We're called hegemons,
accused of building empire.
Civil libertarians
shriek at infringements
of real or imagined rights
at the instigation
of the A.C.L.U.,
mindlessly supported
by the political left.

Granted we have made
serious mistakes,
like feeble explanations
for the invasion of Iraq,
or when we mishandled
the devastating disaster
of hurricane Katrina
for all the world to see.

Yet if we do nothing,
Rwanda, Darfur,
other genocides
that visit the helpless
will continue,
while the U.N. convenes,
deliberates at length,
but is prevented

from taking action
by Russia or China,
intent on their own agenda,
unconcerned
with peace on earth.

Headlines

Oil giants crumble.
Pakistan in turmoil.
Iran launches satellite.
Suicide bombings
in Iraq,
Afghanistan.
Russian troops hunker
near helpless Georgia.
Drug wars in Mexico.
Protesters in China
are disappeared.
From across the world
we learn of horrors
almost immediately,
electronically,
adding to anxiety
that seems to grow and grow,
another fringe benefit
of globalization.

Empire State Building

Your midtown thrust
in depression days
proudly proclaimed
to frightened folk
a writ of stone and steel,
a challenge to the world
that America,
a nation of grabbers
always eager to acquire
the lands of others,
was constructing a tower
that would look down
on the works of man
and dominate the future.

And as you rose,
outstripping other buildings
that had their turn
once the tallest,
your ascent was faster
than any skyscraper before,
yet you did not gloat
as you soared over
lesser cousins,
as the nurtured laborers
high above Manhattan streets
tested the city limits
on precarious perches,
I-beams hovering in space.

How city dwellers gasped
when they looked up
at the distant workers
dining al fresco,
comfortably seated
on your skeleton,
passing the mustard
with casual aplomb,
immortalized for all time
on black and white film
that captured the dazzling grins
of anonymous toilers
in a moment of triumph
over lesser mortals below.

You could not know
that you would reign supreme
longer than any structure
since the Great Pyramid,
the Tower of Babel,
in the melting pot metropolis
that boasted, one at a time,
the tallest buildings
of the twentieth century.
Then when your turn came
to be deposed by a newer upstart,
you lost neither stature, nor grandeur,
accepting your replacement
by the Twin Towers
with a weary dignity.

If a building has a soul,
yours is modest and austere.
You never lost your composure
as rivals outgrew you
and you overlooked
dynamically changing Manhattan
with a benevolent gaze,
until that fateful day
when hateful terrorists
crashed the planes
into the defenseless towers,
leaving you once again
the biggest kid on the block,
forever mourning
the loss of your neighbor.

Great Beginnings

There is a pleasure in the pathless woods.
I saw a staring virgin stand.
Un coup de dès jamais n'abolira le hasard.
Let us go then you and I.

As we become more sophisticated
in electronic communications,
radio, television, internet,
the wonder of words begins to fade,
obscured by pictorial images
that may have been manipulated,
but require little explanation.

So what if we don't know if it's live,
it no longer matters to most of us,
conditioned to accept what we're shown
as a reasonable facsimile
for whatever goes on in the world.

A picture once was worth a thousand words,
but has recently been devalued
due to computer technology
that can alter size, shape, color, time,
add or remove individuals,
actually remake the visual world
until we don't know what to believe.

Those of us who still care
for the fate of our country,
the future of humanity,
are dangerously imperiled
by threats of mass destruction,
made more complicated
since we no longer trust what we see
and have heard the lies already,
heard them all,
till human voices wake us
from dreams of extinction.

Brute Force

Murder always occupied
a prominent place
in the community,
carried out for gain, god,
political ambitions,
military adventures,
madness in time of war,
or one of the deadly sins.
A recent innovation
has become widespread
of murder by spurned suitors,
or psychotic rages unleashed
on schools, churches, the workplace,
even shopping centers,
which threatens the ganglia
of consumer culture
and reveals we're unaware
of the seething torments
driving some to despair
who renounce anguished lives,
but generally include
innocent bystanders.

Orbit

When day is done
the sun straggles off
on its beneficent arc
that neither starts nor stops,
a spatial coincidence
allowing life on earth
brief continuation.

Progress

Bombs exploding,
buildings burning,
cities in flames,
Jerusalem, 1187,
Constantinople, 1453,
Vienna, 1683,
Missalongi, 1824,
ferocious assaults
on the centers
of civilization
that should remind us
the rule of law,
protected by the gun,
often is the only hope
of preserving tenuous
human existence.

Dependency

For many years
our way of life
was the Tao of oil,
that heated our homes,
fueled our cars,
was used so much
we never thought
we were addicted.
Now that we are hooked,
strung out,
dependent,
the pushers have gone mad,
driven by greed
beyond all reason,
threatening to leave us
trapped in darkness.

Encroachment

So the big, bad Russians
may be on the move
threatening to devour
a piece of Europe
and again will test
Europe's resolve
to resist aggression,
too comfortable
with the euro
to risk their possessions
in a dangerous fight.
So they will talk and talk
while the big, bad Russians
march through Georgia,
but hopefully will stop
before gobbling up Turkey.

Light at the End of . . .

In thirty years or so,
barring the unforeseen,
we will forget Iraq
as we forgot Vietnam,
the war that convulsed
a confused land
immersed in a struggle
with an evil empire
for global mastery.

Youth opposed the draft.
Liberals opposed war.
Anarchists opposed all.
Our successes were brief
and failures magnified
by friends and enemies
in a distant conflict
purporting to resist
communist aggression.

Our motives were clear,
to stop Saddam Hussein
from obtaining weapons
of mass destruction,
so we launched an attack
that accomplished our goals.
Suddenly we were left
to rebuild a nation
fallen into chaos.

We made many mistakes,
but there was little help
from those we had saved
from the grip of fascism,
the rule of communism,
who offered criticism,
but refused to assist
in establishing order.

The Mideast will never be
an outpost of democracy,
or so our erstwhile allies said
snug inside their euro bed,
leaving us the thankless chore
of a nation to restore.

Yet our troops are volunteers,
not conscripted legionaries,
or jackbooted storm troopers
goose-stepping in their conquests.
We haven't installed a proxy
who is dancing to our tune.

We enabled the Iraqis
to elect a government
that represents the people,
at least some of the people,
some of the time,
in a region where elections,
if they bother to hold them,
are decided by leaders
without the consent of . . .

Perhaps our government
has unscrupulous designs
on vital Mideast oil
that we're dependent on,
since the lords of profit
who dominate our land
refuse to allow
nuclear power plants
that could provide
cheap electricity,
but will diminish the need
for huge amounts of oil.

Someday our citizens
may reject the system
that consigns their children
to a life of oil dependency
while others wallow in luxury,
if we find leaders
to heal us from consumption.

Globalization

Those who can
participate.
Those who can't
languish in poverty,
forced to rely
on crime or drugs
for subsistence.
Others must accept
a reduced lifestyle,
which reveals the failure
of the promised dream
that inspired millions,
now left behind
because they can't adapt
to the Information Age.

Resourceful

Long ago
we killed whales
for their oil
that lit the lamps
of a dim world.
Illumination
has come to many,
but never enough,
so we make war
to light the lamps
of a harsh world
that fears darkness.

Battered Republic

Doubts arise
if the fragile system
of our battered republic
can manage to endure
the desertion of capital,
the growing losses
of homes, earnings,
basic security,
by a nation founded
on acquisition
that may not survive
the denial of expectation.

Paradox II

Democracy includes
denial of shelter
to homeless families,
eminent domain rulings
for private enterprise
that evict homeowners,
the right to make a fortune
at the expense of others,
free speech for some,
clubs for opposing views.

Across this frightened land
ethnic and racial tensions
still threaten to divide us
when the melting pot
doesn't melt fast enough.
We raise the tower of Babel,
as foreign languages
are not renounced for English,
building a land of confusion
awaiting Balkanization.

Across our divided land
the rich become richer
the poor become poorer,
while our leaders chide nations
for failures of human rights,
oblivious to the millions

of undernourished children
in the good old USA,
deprived of their rights.

We have painfully awakened
from the American dream
that promised hope to many,
now arbitrarily withdrawn
by the servants of profit.

Evolving Education

So many youths
are alienated
from our schools,
the only institutions
with any chance
to alter mind-sets
dangerously shaped
by neglect in the home,
TV violence,
lures of the street.

The lost find comfort
on the Internet.

As resentment grows
because they didn't get
what they wanted,
or got what they didn't want,
they channel their efforts
into plans of revenge
on teachers and classmates,
hated rejecters,
deserving retribution.

Future War

Our troops trudged Baghdad streets,
rode armored vehicles
expecting the sniper's shot,
dreading improvised bombs.

There were no great battles,
dramatic engagements,
just the ongoing struggle
with elusive enemies.

Generals and admirals
prefer decisive clashes,
that defeat the foe
with advanced weaponry.

Long wars of attrition
drain the well of endurance
of leaders and people,
confused as to why we fight.

Generals and admirals
don't like peacekeeping missions,
or nation-building missions,
because they lack clarity.

Many think war is evil
and resist the call to arms
from imperialists
exploiting the world.

Yet in dangerous places
even the most liberal
are glad to see a policeman
patrolling the neighborhood.

But there are no parades for cops
for keeping our streets safe
and those who do their duty
no longer feel respected.

Diagnosis

Dangerous symptoms
are quickly discovered
in apprehensive examinations
that painfully reveal
clogging arteries
that when healthy
should allow
the flow of oil
to the industrial body,
but are being blocked
by convenient laws
of supply and demand
that make some rich,
make others suffer.

Shadows

Tomorrow rushes
at a breakneck pace
hastening us daily
to isolation,
despite the promise
of the Internet
for connectivity.
Our expectations
will fade into darkness
when we lose power.

To Rejected Suitors Who Can't Take No for an Answer

Subtract yourself from life.
You won't be missed,
since you are removed
from redeeming value
to the human race.

You're not significant
like weapons of mass destruction,
natural disaster,
terrorism,
yet you further erode
a woman's rights
by refusing to accept
you are not wanted.

Your poverty is revealed
when you murder a woman
and innocent bystanders
just because she rejected you.

Our society has failed you,
otherwise your life
wouldn't be so valueless,
but we fail the women
shot, stabbed, strangled,
because they dared say no.

Survival

The birds come each morning
and I feed them,
blue jays, doves, finches,
seducible to tameness
in mankind's old pattern
of conquering nature
that I always resist.
I do not pet, coax, comfort,
but often wonder
if I am weakening them
by providing sustenance.
As we further destroy
the frail environment
with concrete, toxins,
other corrosives,
always encroaching
on diminishing habitat,
I often wonder
if I am violating
the harsh laws of survival
by providing sustenance.

Harsh Change

As we go global
those who benefit
cheer the new system
that will bring them
prosperity.

Those left behind
grumble, curse, complain
while they are losing
jobs, homes, hope,
without compensation.

It's hard to deny
that globalism will be
the way of the future,
moved by the Internet
across all borders.

Yet those left behind
are victims of change,
cruelly abandoned
when they couldn't adapt
quickly enough.

No Saviors

As the world grows smaller
narrowed by money
and the Internet,
there are no guardians
of the weak and helpless.
In this rapacious life
those who can, accumulate
heaps of goods, services,
while others struggle
to eke a meager living
in inhospitable lands.
As the means of survival
diminish dangerously
for imperiled millions,
the wealthy consume tomorrows,
discarding the needy
who lack redeeming value.

The End of . . .

The last sunset
cannot be imagined,
its nuclear palette
indescribable,
whether in crude daubs,
commercial blots,
feeble words,
all attempting
the delaying song
before conclusion.

Paradox III

Once in the land of freedom
just before the Civil War,
a political party
emerged in the land,
the Know-Nothings.
Many flocked to their banner
because they proclaimed
contempt and intolerance
for arriving immigrants.
They won local elections,
supported by those who feared
a threat to their way of life
from alien newcomers.

Not even the blood of war
erased our differences,
yet Know-Nothings departed
and the nation staggered on.
Then Know-Somethings took over
and the nation moved forward,
fueled by new immigration,
embracing expansion.

For a while we seemed to flirt
with creating an empire,
occupying foreign lands,
subjecting native peoples
to undemocratic rule.

But another great war
made us rich and powerful
and we freed subject peoples,
except economically,
as we controlled
much of the world's wealth.

Then rivalry expanded
between the super powers
and we confronted each other
across the entire globe,
threatening obliteration,
terrifying our people.
Then Know-It-Alls emerged
and outshouted everyone
with voices of righteousness
that made the frightened forget
they merely pronounced opinions,
not solutions for problems.

Then the clamors of the crowd
silenced voices of reason
that couldn't convince the people
of dangers lurking everywhere.
So the prophets of deceit
enlisted the media,
who aired tacit approval
of *turn on, tune in, drop out,*
as the purveyors of decay
sought control of our future.

And we were a conflicted land
with rockets aiming everywhere,
while our leaders lacked wisdom
and our people went astray
in a complicated world
that easily confused us,
with the only certainties
droned by academics
secure in sheltered campuses,
or glamorous spokespersons
braying on television.

We do not know how to trust,
conditioned to believe
in appealing public personae,
and follow those who promise
to create a better future,
but are careful to avoid
details of how to do it.
We have abundant problems
with very few solutions,
while the troubles in this life
multiply continuously.

We will have dim tomorrows
unless we find new answers
to questions that are dismissed
by the avid manipulators
of ambitious politicians,
eager to get elected
to exercise their egos

in the national spotlight,
self-appointed shepherds,
however unqualified,
dangerous in their greed.

When our new leader fails
to save us from the perils
confronting us everywhere
we will decline and submerge
into second world squalor,
unless we create a council
of our best and brightest
from public and private life,
who develop a plan
to halt the slide to collapse
that erodes our will to survive.

We the people have little choice
but to rely on candidates
who may or may not be worthy
and the only way we'll find out
will be after they mislead us,
another glaring weakness
of elective democracy.

Fixed Positions

Tyrannies demand
strict obedience
from their citizens
and will kill anyone
who tries to defy them.

Anarchists demand
unlimited freedom
from government restraint
and will kill anyone
who tries to control them.

Terrorists demand
numerous restrictions
on nations of consent
and will kill anyone
who tries to resist them.

Democracies display
one standard at home
another abroad
and will kill anyone
who tries to dispute them.

Denial Is Cheaper

Barren stretches
of the Atlantic Ocean
the Pacific Ocean,
recently expanded,
match warming trends
in the same regions.

This duplicates a pattern
scientists predict
occurs in global warming,
warm surface waters
block upswellings
of nutrient-filled water
necessary to support
plankton, other marine life.

Corporations, government
won't allocate cash
to repair damaged seas,
blind to the threat to life.
It's easier to deny
harmful effects
of global warming
than to lose profits
saving the oceans.

Astral Gap

Using radio pictures
astronomers discovered
a huge hole in the universe
without stars or galaxies,
or mysterious dark matter,
so they decided
it was a giant void.
Holes in the universe
probably occur
when the force of gravity
from areas of space with bigger mass
attracts matter from less dense areas.
Scientists won praise
for discovering something
that turned out to be nothing.

Art History

The earliest art in caves
was elemental in nature,
the hunt, primitive physics,
the basics of survival.

As man evolved, so did art,
passing through many stages
with religion and warfare
the primary subjects.

Then the French Revolution
executed patrons of the arts
and artists needed new markets,
so they glorified the people.

But art was still recognizable,
despite Impressionist blurring,
until treacherous cubists
smashed traditional forms.

That was confusing enough
for bewildered collectors,
then Kandinsky finished them off
by removing realism.

The brushes of art moved faster
with rapidly changing styles
and Abstract Expressionists
splattered our understanding.

An enterprising monkey
became a wealthy painter
by splashing paint on canvas
and signing it Jackson Rhesus.

New schools of art came and went
quickly and to such acclaim
that buyers needed experts
to tell them what they liked.

The former boundaries of art
were irrevocably shattered
and artists offered grotesqueries
to a culturally challenged public.

Now dead animals, artifacts,
human excrement, are scooped up
by the purchasers of fashion,
eager to make an art statement.

Critics no longer have standards,
lauding the most absurd efforts
of anyone doing anything,
no matter how silly or sterile.

One artist aspires to pile
390,500 oil barrels
500 feet high,
in an Arabian desert.

This monument would be permanent,
a metaphor of emptiness
that would obviously reflect
the current perception of art.

Night Patrol

The sand clogs our goggles.
It is difficult to see,
more difficult to breathe.
The heat of day is gone
and in this tiny village
on the edge of the desert
we give thanks for thermal underwear.
The squad is spread out
and we move cautiously,
fearing improvised explosive devices
placed there by the same faces
that smile at us in daylight.
Al-Qaeda hasn't used night vision goggles yet,
so we're not worried about snipers,
but we're still alert. It's our asses.
We've learned the hard way
only to think ahead in minutes,
so we don't count how long
until we're back in the tents,
another night survived
in war-torn Iraq.

Innovative Love

The eternal triangle
between two rivals
for a desirable woman
has been reinvented
for the Information Age.
While surfing the Internet,
an addictive diversion
for underutilized minds,
two men were welcomed
by an enticing woman
who built a relationship
using remote control
that provoked one suitor
to murder the other.
An investigation revealed
the enterprising woman
used her daughter's web page
to pose as an eighteen-year-old
and lured the distant victims
to a violent end,
deceiving them
electronically.

Across the Universe

NASA sent the Beatles song
"Across the Universe,"
to the North Star, Polaris,
431 light years away
via the Deep Space Network
of multiple antennas.
One of the surviving Beatles
sent his love to the aliens,
leaving us to wonder
what they might send back.

Paradox IV

Bombs explode in Lebanon,
Afghanistan, Palestine,
most often in Iraq,
many other places
as I sit on my terrace
in relative comfort,
an illusion of safety,
while I watch the doves fight
for control of the feeder.

Estranged Kin

Other than hellish heat,
crushing atmosphere
of carbon dioxide,
corrosive clouds
of sulfuric acid,
Venus is a lot like Earth.
It's about the same size,
the same mass,
the same composition.
But don't plan on moving soon
despite tempting offers
from expansive realtors,
since surface temperatures
exceed 800 degrees.
Investors are better off waiting
for lower real estate prices
when global warming
completes greenhouse effect,
transforming Earth
into sister Venus.

The Tyranny of Oil

A greasy commodity
is throttling the world
in a crude conspiracy
by producers, cartels,
energy companies,
many arid countries
lacking other valuables,
and treacherous hordes
of greedy investors
profiting from the chaos
of market driven prices
rising and falling daily,
devouring the consumer.

Urban Oasis

I sit on my terrace
in mid-town Manhattan
removed from city strife
and find relief
from brick, glass, concrete,
unnatural materials
perpetuating abuse
of the environment.
The honks, sirens, screams
become more remote
as I console myself
with flowers, trees, birds.

More Light

Once mankind lived
a regulated life;
awaken at dawn,
eat a meager meal,
hunt or gather all day,
hopefully gorge at dusk
and sleep the night away,
troubled by fearful dreams.

Then we discovered fire
and when it became dark
we could see each other
and we talked, bragged, schemed,
so when we went to bed
the day had been richer.

We developed the need
for illumination;
torch, candle, lantern
barely lit the night,
until gas lamps
burned so bright
that all our desires
seemed to be in sight.

When electric bulbs arrived
we sacrificed tranquility
on the altar of more light.

Intonations of Dead Presidents

I. How fortunate I am
    that no one remembers
    when I was president
    and did not prevent
    the Civil War.
    How citizens reviled
    former president Bush
    and called him a monster,
    but he was the people's choice.
    Selective forgetting
    is another comfort
    that citizens invoke
    in a democracy.

II. History treats me well,
    overlooking the fact
    that I almost destroyed
    the entire planet
    in a nuclear war.
    President Obama
    may have charisma,
    but is less experienced
    then I ever was
    and only desperation
    compelled his selection
    to lead the nation.

III. I tried to bring world peace
and though intelligent,
I was too ignorant
of the way of the world.
Events overwhelmed me
shattering my ideals
and I allowed public clamor
to lead us into war.
Issues now are sound bytes,
making it easier
for leaders to fool
the gullible public.

Us or Them

The defense of *We the people*
from oppression by the rich,
abuse from the powerful,
exploitation by the ruthless
in the savvy Internet age
has confused our best and brightest
who don't know who rules the nation
and all their liberal courses
and indulgences in the arts
do not confront the true crisis,
that the many will be consumed
by the appetites of the few.
As callous as aristocrats
of pre-revolutionary France
detached from the suffering
of those below them,
our own privileged caste
is indifferent to the fate
of those who lose homes, jobs,
future security,
the abandoned,
who cannot find
a champion *of the people*
to protect their rights.

One More Darfur Disaster

The ongoing civil war,
one of Africa's longest
and deadliest conflicts,
between non-Arab rebels
and the Arab dominated
Sudanese Government,
has devastated Darfur.
United Nations peacekeepers
replaced an African force,
but their convoy was ambushed
by Janjaweed militia
on camels and horseback,
who snuck up on a detachment
of Nigerian peacekeepers
and robbed them of cash and weapons.
The Nigerians didn't fight back,
claiming they were outnumbered,
once again demonstrating
the failure of the U.N.
to even protect itself.

Unpredictable

What will the future bring?
A question posed by many,
seers, singers, poets,
ambitious politicians
hungering success.
Pundit historians
are quick to explain
theories of tomorrow
based on yesterday's events,
as some plod on
hoping for the best,
while others consume,
devouring the present.

A Benefit of The Information Age

The Mine Safety Administration
approved a wireless tracking system
to locate miners trapped underground.
The technology was developed
by the Venture Corporation
located in Singapore,
an island nation without mines,
which may be the reason why
they took so long to make it.
This doesn't mean mines are safer,
dangers of the deep pit remain,
but now we'll find the corpses faster,
guided electronically.

Paradox V

The USA has done more
to benefit the world,
especially the poor,
than any great power
in recorded history.
We've done some bad things,
often conspicuously,
yet despite our faults
we have assisted many,
but still are as hated
as ancient Rome.

Dead Zones, A Poetic Explanation

A dangerous process begins
when nitrogen-rich nutrients
from agriculture and sewage
spill into coastal waters
by way of rivers and streams
and stimulate the growth
of photosynthetic plankton
on the surface of coastal waters.
When organisms decay
they sink to the bottom
and are decomposed by microbes
that consume large amounts of oxygen.
As oxygen levels drop
at the bottom of the sea
most animals cannot survive.
Dependents of the sea,
human and animal alike,
suffer the consequences
of diminishing food supplies
as our oceans become sterile.

Invocation

Gunfire on the corner.
Again.
The Americans patrol the streets.
The sight of them offends me.
I think of my AK-47
hidden under the floor boards.
Yet the Shiite militia
is even more hateful,
crowing like kings of the dunghill
now that Saddam no longer rules.
So I must endure degradation
and hope my Sunni brothers
will not befriend the Americans,
who would undo us with democracy.

Who Will Feed Us?

Before we were America
we bitterly resisted
impositions by England,
until the revolution.
Then many colonists
opposed the call to war,
remaining loyal to the crown.
This set an early pattern
of citizen contrariness
bulwarked by the constitution,
the magical document
that protects and burdens.

War was always popular,
until the media rebelled
showing the horrors of Vietnam
live, in color, 24/7,
punishing the public
who thought war was sanitary
and nice American boys
didn't commit atrocities.
The media rarely showed
enemy atrocities,
deciding that the public
was much too sensitive
to see the enemy's abuses,
only American abuses.

So we blamed the military
for being mercenary soldiers
serving an evil empire,
and dissenters have louder voices
and more rabid convictions
than supporters of the state
and they always feel secure
with constitutional protection.
So what if we were defeated.
It allowed the left to gloat
that they were right.

But the world has changed
since the sophists of surrender
asserted we are always wrong.
Terror has invaded our shores
killing innocent civilians,
whose rights were violated
in a new kind of war
from those threatened
by countries of consent
and only personal tragedy
may alert dissenters
of dangers to democracy
that might force us
to lose our resolution
and like once courageous Spain
yield to terrorist blackmail.

Special Education

Birds and bees
once were used
as teaching tools
for our kiddies
to prepare them
for maturity.
Now children are taught
to read the manuals
of AK-47s
and get graduation gifts
of suicide vests.

Prognosis

Unless we find remedies,
a doubtful prospect
since oil interests
won't allow substitution
and prefer
systemic disaster
to giving up
excess profits,
we will succumb
to terminal disease
from limited supplies
of industrial vaccine.

Whither Goest?

More than eight billion miles away
Voyager 2 continues its trek
and passed through a sonic boom
of solar wind particles
in our outer solar system.
On August 30th, 2007
the craft registered the speed
of charged particles from the sun
passing at 700,000 MPH,
that slowed to 350,000 MPH,
possibly to wave goodbye.
Then the spacecraft entered
the magnetic bubble
that envelops our solar system,
outward bound on its mission
that will take it who knows where
when it exits the solar system,
perhaps by 2015,
as long as nothing interferes
with a fragile journey.

For Whom the Cash Flows

The New York Times asserts
the rich are getting richer
and the increase in incomes
of the top one percent
exceeded the total income
of the poorest twenty percent.
Now this may surprise many
who believe in democracy,
but it won't shock others
who know capitalism.
After all, whose country is it?
The rich consider it theirs,
because they own so much of it
and if people work harder
for their share of the promised dream
that always seems to elude them,
the rich are ready to say
there are no guarantees in life.

Roadside

Improvised roadside devices
make absolutely no distinction
between the innocent and guilty.
Whoever comes along
at the wrong moment
becomes a sudden target,
a victim of detonation,
murdered without explanation.

What Profiteth

The food supply is shrinking,
the cost of food is soaring,
fewer people will get food,
in the developing world.
The effects of global warming
decreased essential crop yields,
as farming for human consumption
shifted to biofuel crops.
While the world's population grows
demand for grain is increasing,
yet more is used for cattle feed
for upwardly mobile meat-eaters,
pricing the poor out of the market.
The U.N. calls this climate crisis
a result of a recent confluence
of supply and demand factors
that threatens the lives of the poor.
Thus the best way to avoid famine
since the poor can't afford tractors
is the return to neolithic farming.

Madness Agonistes

When the price of oil goes up
consumers cry at the cost
draining their meager income,
limiting participation
in the global supermarket
offering goods and services
from every corner of the earth.
Most Americans feel betrayed
when they can no longer afford
to buy what they want to buy,
once an unspoken covenant
between a people of consent
and their elected government.

Now that we're dependant
on the black juice of mother earth,
those who control the quantity
of industrial serum
that nourishes our way of life
manipulate delivery
of non-renewable fuel,
causing escalating prices,
curtailing more activities
of our struggling citizens,
including basic nutrition,
loss of homes, jobs, security,
as we're guided towards poverty.

Now that we are hostages
of a limited fossil fuel,
the lunatics who govern us
proposed a crazier idea:
replacing gasoline fuel
with ethanol made from corn.
This way barely fertile acres
tainted by commercial farming
that used toxic additives
are ruthlessly abandoned
when no longer productive,
diminishing the food supply
of cereals and grains.

As our cars rust in garages
and our tables grow empty
we elect bankrupt minds
who delude us with promises
that the frightened believe.
The hope of continuation
will fade with expectations,
unless we make an action plan
that insures survival.
Soon we will be helpless victims,
of the panderers of profit,
consigned to diminished dreams,
while they sail away on mega-yachts.

Global Warming

The weather pattern changes
frequently, erratically,
and meteorologists
with advanced college degrees
make poorer predictions
than the Farmer's Almanac,
once meant for rural readers
who couldn't foresee climate change.

Paradox VI

We are the first to give
in times of disaster,
rushing food, medicine,
technical assistance
to relieve the needy,
yet it's quickly forgotten
as soon as America
does something wrong.

Witchcraft

A gang of young men in Kenya
rampaged through two villages
hunting witches and wizards,
suspected of casting spells
that made bright children dumb.
The gang slit the throats,
or clubbed to death,
eight women, three men,
each over seventy years old,
then burned their bodies.
The Kikuyu blamed the Wakamba.
The Wakamba blamed the Masai.
The Masai sneered at everyone.
But the tribal elders agreed
that someone should be punished
for making children dumber,
so they selected witches.

Rampage

A jealous deputy sheriff,
rejected by his girlfriend,
went to her house,
accused her of dating others
and she demanded he leave.
He returned with an assault rifle,
broke down her door,
opened fire on her friends
attending her party.
He killed six people,
wounded another, then fled.
Hours later, trapped by police,
who couldn't persuade him to surrender,
he shot himself in the head.
The victim's house was demolished,
debris secretly buried
so no one could obtain
a ghoulish souvenir
of an act of madness.

Ravenous Black Hole

The Large Hadron Collider
operating in Geneva
is designed to speed protons,
the building blocks of matter,
then crash them together
to produce tiny fireballs,
miniature versions
of the Big Bang theory.
Concerned critics worry
that the enormous collider
could produce a black hole
that would swallow the Earth.
The safety review
by builders of the machine
assured everyone
there was nothing to fear
and the stars and galaxies
will continue to endure,
unless they're wrong.

Who Will Bear Our Burden?

Not all worries of the world
consume our energy each day,
since there are some we overlook
to insure we remain sane.
Our biggest daily worry
is the leaders of the world
only concern themselves
with temporary issues,
ignoring threats to survival
of the entire human race.
Global warming, climate change,
weapons of mass destruction,
natural disasters,
exhaust our will and wealth,
deplete our reserves
for the endless struggle
of continuation.

Capital Expansion

It is hard to imagine
the world renouncing war,
the useful commodity
of human engineering
that surpasses tooth and claw.
When we threw the first stone,
swung the first club
the arms race began
and investment grew
in mass destruction.

First one enemy was slain,
then families, clans, tribes,
until cities were founded,
which allowed us to destroy
groups of complete strangers,
impersonally.

The tools of war grew bigger
and devastated nations,
but the nature of man
was basically the same,
greedy, cruel, ambitious,
eager to demolish
anything preventing
greater acquisition.

The calls for peace increased
in relative proportion
to the spread of weapons
of mass . . .
but weak voices
were insufficient
to halt development
of new weapons of mass . . .

On our seething planet
narrowed by the Internet,
globalization
is changing the pattern
of traditional exchange,
while old animosities
continue to dominate
policies of nations,
religions, ethnicities,
industriously fueled
by old and new resentments.

As profits grow for some
many are left behind,
victims of poverty
and all the other ills
that beset the helpless,
unable to compete
in the new marketplace,
or the old marketplace,
as we punish children
for the parents' failures.

The mythological curse
on the House of Atreus,
the House of Laius,
were tragic enactments
that punished children
for the sins of the fathers.
But we no longer believe,
at least most of us don't,
in the power of a curse,
yet we cannot explain
why the children suffer,
who are victims of the crime
of being born in poverty.

We continue to evolve,
growing bigger and stronger,
reflected in our weapons
that grow bigger and stronger,
but we may not grow smarter,
which will be a major threat
to the hope of existence
for terrified millions
who cannot control
their own destinies.

Hard Times

The American Dream
was built on oil
and as we awaken
from years of comfort
losing jobs, homes,
security,
we must accept,
before it's too late,
that our dependency
on ample flow
has been betrayed
at home and abroad,
crumbling the foundation
of our rusting land.

Matriculation

Two sullen boys
rejected by their peers
gave up video games
for plans of destruction
that entertained them
as they savored vengeance.
Parents and teachers
betrayed these children,
who couldn't accept
isolation,
frustration,
failure to connect
to a meaningful life.
When they couldn't get
what they wanted,
because of insufficient
opportunities,
abilities,
they put their few resources
into preparations
for harsh retribution
on uncaring classmates.

Anthropology

On state occasions
trumpets sound:
"Hail to the Chief,"
which sounds more tribal
than republican,
but reminds us
a chief must lead,
despite the democratic burden
of institutions designed
for a simpler age.
Chiefs once decided,
often seeking counsel
from shamans, seers,
medicine men,
other interveners
between rash action
and good policy.
Then they hunted,
made war,
moved the village,
planted corn,
and didn't have to deal
with smog, pollution,
ozone layers, lawsuits,
all the accoutrements
of modern society.
They knew what should be done,
went ahead and did it

and didn't fear term limits,
unlike our current chiefs
who may not lead us
to better tomorrows.

Distant Ventures

The Mars rover flew far,
but now crawls slowly.
The Hubble Telescope
peeks, peers, pries
into distant secrets
of the galaxy,
but will soon go blind.
Various packages
orbit the solar system
and a few have ventured
out into the galaxy
with no humans aboard.
The space station
grows and grows,
the most expensive habitat
on or off our planet.
When launchings cease,
the penthouse in the sky
will wither and die,
the last space outpost
of bold endeavors,
sadly abandoned
by human decline.

Paranoid? Or . . .

I look out my window
and the sun is shining,
the trees sway in the breeze,
the doves wait for their seed.
Everything seems normal,
but I still cannot relax,
awaiting the disaster
that I always expect.

A Moral Tale A La Shelley

I met a merchant from an oil-poor land,
who said: "Two vast and rusting derricks stand
that once produced an almost endless flow
that made the engines of the planet go.
Now nothing remains but desolation."
Sand has covered the hopes of a nation
that consumed its wealth on useless trifles,
then lost it to automatic rifles.

A Turbulent Bird

The V-22 Osprey,
an aircraft that flies like a plane,
takes off and lands like a helicopter,
was designed to ferry Marines
into and out of combat.

The craft's unusual design
and powerful propellers
make it vulnerable
to its own downdraft
and crashing to the ground.
In order to prevent this
the Osprey must operate
with severe flight restrictions
that require it to land slowly,
making it a better target
for enemy fire.

The Osprey failed many tests,
so the Pentagon concluded
that its problems were caused
by extended exposure
to the desert environment,
the very same environment
where our Marines fight in Iraq.

The project was spread over forty states,
giving members of congress

from both parties
a stake in development,
for the jobs created
translate into votes.
More than one hundred members formed
"Tiltrotor Technology Coalition"
and lobbied until it was funded.

The generals, CEOs, and congress
won another costly victory
from the ignorant public,
but they won't fly into combat
with our volunteer troops
on this dangerously flawed bird
that costs one hundred million
dollars each
and can be shot down
by a single enemy
with a cheap hand-held missile.

The Madness of Our Times

A man who takes his gun to work
and kills his fellow employees
is not much different
than a terrorist,
who surprises us
with brutal violence.
We're horrified when terror strikes,
briefly react, quickly forget,
go on with our chores
and ignore the war on terror
until it impacts on our lives,
just as when a man goes postal,
temporarily shocking us
from conditioned apathy.

Other Means

The war on terror doesn't take place
on traditional battlefields
hallowed by the blood of armies.

The clash of nations is departing.

The war on terror doesn't involve
oppressed freedom fighters
seeking to replace tyranny.

Their flag cloaks the drug trade.

The war on terror targets civilians,
instilling dread that their nation
can no longer protect them.

We must wait to see
if democracy
will survive the erosive
war on terror.

Cruel Capitalism

As profits soar for some,
others lose their homes,
consigned to poverty
by a system that has forgotten
the meaning of "for the people."

When big business fails
congress rushes to support
a costly bailout,
claiming it's for the good
of the economy.

Thousands of people
consigned to homelessness
are part of the economy,
but aren't assisted
by a system "of the people."

When a handful lose their homes
through extravagance
we ignore their suffering,
which is considered
personal tragedy.

When millions are displaced
this disrupts a nation,
as well as the economy,
yet they are still neglected
by a government "by the people."

Paradox VII

If beauty lies
in the eyes
of the beholder,
does it disappear
when the eyes are closed,
or when we stop looking?

Can beauty exist
without mankind
to appreciate it,
or will it continue
without an audience,
aesthetically intact?

Imminent Event

The more literate we become
the more history teaches us
that empires don't endure,
dissolve in suffering
of the people once sheltered
by comforting institutions.

When empires of the past
fell with a mighty fall
life on earth continued
and new civilizations
arose to maintain order,
provide stability,
necessary conditions
for human endeavors.

When the air becomes tainted,
the oceans become sterile,
the land becomes exhausted,
will we perish by millions
from natural disasters,
weapons of mass destruction,
horrific epidemics?

The evidence would be clear
in an honest courtroom
and we would be found guilty
of destroying tomorrow.

Mired in ignorance, greed,
we refuse to change the ways
that may lead us to extinction.

We barely acknowledge
those who urge initiatives
to act before it's too late
to preserve dwindling resources
that protect the environment,
provide us existence.

Our feeble efforts
are insufficient to halt
the inevitable end
of life as we know it
for those who can't afford
modern caves of survival.

We may already have reached
the point of no return
for the future of the earth,
but there may still be time,
before calamity
removes the human race
from its hoped-for destiny,
to repair spaceship earth,
continue our journey
and people the galaxy.

A Way of Life

The bigger
intimidate the smaller.
The stronger
abuse the weaker.
The oppressed rarely know
how to unite
against tyranny.
This is our system
of education
that leaves many of us
lacking protection
from bullies,
becoming victims
succumbing to terror.

A Progressive Nation

We once led the world
in producing
oil, steel, food,
many other things.
Now we lead the world
in producing
arts graduates,
service jobs,
advanced weaponry.
The flight of capital,
the disastrous brain drain,
the loss of promised hope,
will cause a barren land.

Hierarchy

The doves sit in the tree
afraid to come to the terrace
because big dove is here
and will peck any bird
who tries to share the feeder.
When he's eaten enough
the other birds land
and the struggle begins,
the feathers fly,
in the age old conflict
for dominance.

One Solution

Our troubled world
never knew peace
always beset
by bloody conflict,
animal,
vegetable,
even mineral
struggling for gain,
the right to exist,
lebensraum.
The dream of peace
by the frightened,
the idealists,
may only arrive,
at least on earth,
if we send the aggressive
deep into space,
where they'll wreak havoc
on unwary aliens,
in a galactic rampage
that may bring
peace on earth,
unless aggrieved aliens
retaliate.

Erosive Streets

Illusions of safety
are easily shattered
by endless disasters,
while the anonymity
of big city life
makes it easy to ignore
the sufferings of others.

Oh, Too Human

Terror's relentless face
smiles at destruction
justifying itself
with claims of higher aims,
yet terrorists don't dare admit
they're trapped on the wheel of hate
and are thrilled by savage acts
until they're consumed by fate.

Dereliction of Duty

Self-appointed caretakers
of the unconsulted earth
violated the contract
between mankind and nature
to share abundant resources
and leave some for another day.
Instead we consumed madly,
exhausting the storehouse for all,
destroying what we couldn't carry.
Unlike other species
we perceive the future,
yet have blinded ourselves
to the threat to continuation.

City of Compassion

Homeless families with children
are denied beds for the night
at a homeless intake center,
because of a new policy
that forbids granting shelter
in last–minute emergencies
to families who were ruled
ineligible for benefits.
Diligent bureaucrats
blamed several families
for causing their decision,
claiming they abused the system.
The same officials
go home to comforts,
completely unconcerned
with the welfare of children,
innocent victims
punished for sins of the parents.

Ecology

The signature of man
is indelibly placed
on the works of man.
The bountiful Earth
was brutally ravaged
by a transient horde
seeking civilization,
in a relentless war
on the natural world.
In boundless ignorance
we polluted our nest
beyond redemption,
recent dreams of green
mere illusions,
invoked too little, too late
in the inevitable tide
carrying us to extinction.

Service

The living must forget the dead
if they would continue living,
but memories that bound them
should have a token remembrance.
A marker, milestone, monolith,
will only be appropriate
for those who distinguished themselves
and gained public recognition.
For most who made scant impression
their fate is inevitable,
lingering a faint moment,
becoming indistinct,
an inactive presence
who toiled much, accomplished little,
gradually fading away,
barely contributing
to continuation.

A Matter of . . .

Nature is under assault
from its greatest enemy,
man, the vicious invader.
It remains to be seen
whether nature's weapons,
earthquake, hurricane, flood,
are sufficient to defend
fortress earth
against the rash intruder,
before he destroys everything.

Ode to Continuation

I do not know what tomorrows
I will live long enough to see,
but our future preparations
have been made inadequately.
The perils that endanger us,
magnified by technology,
will only be survivable
if we avert catastrophe.

Poems from *Perceptions* have appeared in: *Perspectives Magazine*, *Ex Cathedra Literary Magazine*, *South Jersey Underground*, *The Stray Branch*, *Spark Bright*, *The Scruffy Dog Review*, *Seven Circle Press*, *Thirty First Bird Review*, *Poet's Ink Review*, *Carcinogenic Poetry* (Virogray Press), *The Virtuous Mimicry*, *Mobius Poetry Magazine*, *Poets For Living Waters*, *Fair Trade Journal*, *Heavy Hands Ink*, *The Democratic Publishing Project*, *Garbaj* (Atlantean Publishing), *Bluestem Magazine*, *The Fine Line*, *The Scarlet Sound*, *Unshod Quills*, *The Rockford Review*, *Crack the Spire*, Atlantean Publishing (chapbook: *Iraq Monologues*), *Speech Therapy Poetry*, *Jellyfish Whispers* (Kind of a Hurricane Press), *Contemporary Literary Review India*, *Weasel and Gun*, *The Writers Wastebasket*, *Bard* (Atlantean Publishing), *The Redbridge Review*, *The Blue Hour Magazine*, *Pyrokinection* (Kind of a Hurricane Press), *Decanto Magazine* (Masque Publishing), *Conceit Magazine*, *Blue Fifth Review*, and *Revival*.

About the Author

Gary Beck has spent most of his adult life as a theater director. He has had numerous published works including *Days of Destruction*, *Expectations*, and his novel, *Flawed Connections*, published by Black Rose Writing. Gary has also had several original plays and translations produced off Broadway, in New York City, where he currently resides.

www.ingramcontent.com/pod-product-compliance
Lightning Source LLC
Chambersburg PA
CBHW051345040426
42453CB00007B/412